EASY G

AMERICAN
SIGN
LANGUAGE

LEARN THE BASICS FAST

edited by Lora Heller

FALL RIVER PRESS

New York

FALL RIVER PRESS

New York

An Imprint of Sterling Publishing Co., Inc.
1166 Avenue of the Americas
New York, NY 10036

ISBN 978-1-4351-6457-4

Distributed in Canada by Sterling Publishing Co., Inc.
c/o Canadian Manda Group, 664 Annette Street
Toronto, Ontario, Canada M6S 2C8
Distributed in the United Kingdom by GMC Distribution Services
Castle Place, 166 High Street, Lewes, East Sussex, England BN7 1XU
Distributed in Australia by NewSouth Books
45 Beach Street, Coogee, NSW 2034, Australia

For information about custom editions, special sales, and premium
and corporate purchases, please contact Sterling Special Sales
at 800-805-5489 or specialsales@sterlingpublishing.com.

Manufactured in Canada

2 4 6 8 10 9 7 5 3 1

www.sterlingpublishing.com

Cover design by Igor Satanovsky
Interior design by Bruce McKillip

CONTENTS

INTRODUCTION

THE BASICS

American Sign Language (ASL) is a visual, gesture-based system of communication used by Deaf individuals in the United States and Canada. It is difficult to estimate the number of people who communicate with ASL as their primary language, but two million is often suggested.

In 1815, Thomas Hopkins Gallaudet went to Europe to study Deaf communications and teaching methods. He met Deaf Frenchman Laurent Clerc, who later became the first Deaf educator in the United States. For that reason, today'giraffes ASL is based on French Sign Language, with many of the words originating from French.

ASL is not a universal language, as many countries have their own sign languages. Even within the United States there are regional variations for certain words and phrases; in such cases, this book offers the most common choice of signs for each word or phrase. Although there has been an attempt to internationalize sign language, the effort has met many challenges due to inconsistency of grammatical rules.

Many schools now recognize American Sign Language as a foreign language.

PARTS OF A SIGN

A sign has four parts—handshape, palm orientation, movement, and location.

A sign may also include nonmanual components, such as movements of the face, eyes, head, and/or body posture

Signing Space and Gender Notation
The signing space in which signs are made generally extends from above the head to about waist level, between the shoulders. Most signs are made at or near the head, neck, face, and chest regions so that they are visible to the recipient.

To indicate male or female, some signs can be made in the male region (forehead) or the female region (cheek or chin).

Dominant Hand

ASL uses both hands, but the dominant hand is the signer's writing hand. Instructions that are presented for one hand typically use the right hand but can be reversed for left-handed signers.

Plurals

The signer can denote plural nouns in three main ways:

1. Add a quantity sign (e.g., "four," "many," etc.) to the noun.

2. Make the sign repeatedly.

3. Sign the word or concept once, then point with the pointer finger where the objects would be located.

Verb Tense

In spoken English, verb tense is indicated by conjugation, e.g., "I wrote," "I write," "I will write." In ASL, tense is indicated using time words, e.g., "Yesterday I write," "Now I write," "Later I write."

Negatives

In ASL, sentences are made negative through the addition of negative signs such as "nothing" or "not" (e.g., "unhappy" = "not" + "happy"). Other cues, such as a side-to-side head-shake, are also used to suggest negativity or negation.

ASL vs. Signed English

Although ASL is the primary language of the Deaf in the United States, it is not the only communication system used.

- ASL is made up of a set of conceptual signs, but is not a word-for-word translation of English. ASL has its own grammatical structure, which does not directly translate to English structure. ASL:
  - Does not always indicate past, present, and future tenses.
  - Does not necessarily present words in the order heard.
  - Often drops supporting words (such as "a" and "the").

- Some educational philosophies now promote the use of Signed English, a system in which English is signed verbatim, word-for-word (including verb conjugation and tenses). Some educators believe that Signed English develops English speaking and writing skills better than ASL.

- Pidgin sign is a combination of ASL and Signed English that combines elements of the two approaches.

- For signing purposes, the fingers on the hand are named as follows:

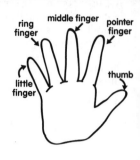

ring finger middle finger pointer finger

little finger thumb

- The directions on this chart use the right hand as the dominant hand. Instructions may be reversed for left-handed interpreters. If reference is not made to a specific hand, the right hand (or dominant signing hand) should be used.

- The instructions for each sign on this chart (aside from the manual alphabet and numbers) follow this format:

[concept/word]

- starting handshape
- movement (if any)
- explanation or rationale behind sign (if any)

Introduction

1 THE MANUAL ALPHABET AND NUMBERS

Alphabet

- right hand open with palm down at chest level
- move hand from left to right while wiggling fingers
- ASL for "fingerspelling"

A		closed fist with thumb extended
B		flat palm with thumb touching pointer finger or extended across fingers, sometimes at an angle
C		a letter C with fingers and thumb
D		a letter D with thumb and three fingers with pointer finger extended upward
E		open fist with thumb curled across palm
F		thumb and pointer forming a circle; remaining fingers extended upward (**hint:** opposite of D)

G		closed fist with pointer finger and thumb extended to side
H		closed fist with pointer and middle fingers extended to side
I		closed fist with little finger extended upward
J		closed fist with little finger extended upward, sweeping a J shape in the air
K		pointer and middle fingers extended at angle with thumb at base of angle (**hint:** extended "arm" and "leg" of the letter K)
L		thumb and pointer finger at a right angle (**hint:** looks like the letter L)
M		pointer, middle, and ring fingers resting on thumb, with little finger tucked
N		pointer and middle fingers resting on thumb, with ring and little fingers tucked
O		all fingers forming an O (**note:** a closed "O" is often used to make concept/word signs and is formed by compressing the fingers together)
P		pointer and middle fingers extended downward (flipped letter K)
Q		pointer finger extended downward (flipped letter G)
R		closed fist with pointer and middle fingers extended and crossed (railroad crossing)

S	closed fist with thumb curled over fingers
T	closed fist with thumb between pointer and middle fingers
U	closed fist with pointer and middle fingers extended upward and touching
V	closed fist with pointer and middle fingers extended upward and separated
W	closed fist with pointer, middle, and ring fingers extended upward and separated
X	closed fist with pointer finger extended and curled
Y	closed fist with thumb and middle fingers extended
Z	closed fist with pointer finger extended, writing a letter Z in the air

0		fingers in O shape
1		closed fist with pointer finger extended (**note:** this sign is often used to make concept/word signs)
2		closed fist with pointer and middle fingers extended and separated (same as letter V)
3		closed fist with extended and separated pointer and middle fingers and thumb (**note:** different from letter W)
4		four fingers extended and separated with thumb across palm
5		all five fingers extended and separated (**note:** this sign is often used to make concept/word signs)
6		tip of thumb to tip of little finger with remaining fingers extended
7		tip of thumb to tip of ring finger with remaining fingers extended
8		tip of thumb to tip of middle finger with remaining fingers extended
9		tip of thumb to tip of pointer finger with remaining fingers extended
10		"A" shape with fist closed and thumb extended, twist (form toward body outward)
11		"S" shape to extended pointer finger, snap pointer finger two times, palm facing in

12		"S" shape to extended pointer and middle fingers, snap fingers two times, palm facing in
13		make "3" shape, fingers bend two or three times
14		make "4" shape, fingers bend two or three times
15		make "5" shape, fingers bend two or three times
16		"A" shape with fist closed and thumb extended with palm facing in, change to tip of thumb to tip little finger with remaining fingers extended outward with palm facing out: "10" + "6"
17		"A" shape with fist closed and thumb extended with palm facing in, change to tip of thumb to tip of ring finger with remaining fingers extended with palm facing out: "10" + "7"
18		"A" shape with fist closed and thumb extended with palm facing in, change to tip of thumb to tip of middle finger with remaining fingers extended with palm facing out: "10" + "8"
19		"A" shape with fist closed and thumb extended with palm facing in, change to tip of thumb to tip of pointer finger with remaining fingers extended with palm facing out: "10" + "9"
20		closed fist with thumb and pointer finger extended, open and close thumb and pointer finger
30		closed fist with thumb and pointer and middle fingers extended, open and close thumb and fingers

40		four fingers extended and separated with thumb across palm, change to closed fist with thumb and pointer and middle fingers extended, open and close: "4" + "0"
50		all five fingers extended and separated, change to closed fist with thumb and pointer and middle fingers extended, open and close: "5" + "0"
60		tip of thumb to tip of little finger with remaining fingers extended, change to closed fist with thumb and pointer and middle fingers extended, open and close: "6" + "0"
70		tip of thumb to tip of ring finger with remaining fingers extended, change to closed fist with thumb and pointer and middle fingers extended, open and close: "7" + "0"
80		tip of thumb to tip of middle finger with remaining fingers extended, change to closed fist with thumb and pointer and middle fingers extended, open and close: "8" + "0"
90		tip of thumb to tip of middle finger with remaining fingers extended, change to closed fist with thumb and pointer and middle fingers extended, open and close: "9" + "0"
100		fingers in "C" shape (C is the Roman numeral for 100; can precede the "C" with "1" shape)
1000		"M" shape with fingertips of right hand resting on palm of left (M is the Roman numeral for 1,000; can precede the "M" with "1" shape)
1,000,000		"M" shape with fingertips of right hand resting on palm of left, strike right hand on left palm (1,000 times 1,000)

2 GREETINGS AND PHRASES

Hello

- "B" hand along right side of head
- deliberate and to the right
- saluting motion

Good-bye

- open hand with fingers extended and pressed together
- bend fingers up and down
- waving goodbye

How are you?

- fingers of both hands at chest, knuckles touching
- flow hands up and out to palms facing up, then extend primary pointer finger forward
- "how" + "you"

I'm fine

- "5" hand with thumb touching chest
- move hand away from chest
- signing "fine" only

What's your name?

- make "your" shape with right hand
- then tap "H" hands twice and then make "what?" shape with inquisitive look on face
- "your" + "name" + "what?"

My name is . . .

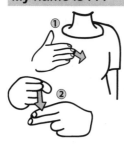

- flat hand touching chest
- touch chest once, tap "H" hands twice
- sign "my" and "name" only, followed by fingerspelling of name

Please

- right hand open on chest
- repeated circular motion
- rubbing heart with pleasure

Thank you

- open hand with tips of fingers on mouth
- move fingers away from mouth
- —

You're welcome

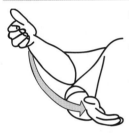

- open hand away from and to the side of body
- sweep hand down toward waist with palm up
- "welcome" only

Excuse me

- fingertips of right hand across open left palm
- brushing motion from heel of hand to fingertips
- brushing away

Yes

- "S" hand
- bent wrist; repeated up-and-down motion
- simulating head nodding

No

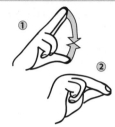

- pointer and middle fingers extended, touching thumb
- two quick open-and-close motions
- "N" + "O" quickly

I'm sorry

- "A" hand on chest
- repeated circular motion
- sorrow of heart

I love you

- closed fist with thumb, pointer, and little fingers extended at chest
- —
- sign makes letters "I", "L", "Y"

Good luck

- hands in "A" positions with extended thumbs pointing upward
- slight movement forward and out
- thumbs up

Huh?

- both palms facing up, arms bent at 90-degree angle
- hunch shoulders and move hands slightly back and forth with inquisitive look on face
- asking gesture

Sign (language)

- hands in "D" positions with pointer fingers pointing in front of chest
- hands make circular pedaling motion in front of chest
- may include signs for "language" (steps 2 and 3)

Happy Birthday

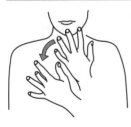

- touch middle finger to chin
- move middle finger down and slightly left to touch heart
- —

3 QUESTION WORDS

Question

- hand in "1" position
- write a question mark in the air
- traces shape of question mark (**note:** used before or after question)

Who?

- place tip of thumb below chin with pointer finger extended
- bend pointer finger twice with inquisitive look on face
- —

What?

- both palms facing up, arms bent at a 90-degree angle
- hunch shoulders and move hands slightly back and forth with inquisitive look on face
- asking gesture

When?

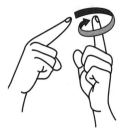

- holds left pointer finger up, palm facing right
- tip of right pointer finger circles the left, clockwise, and then rests on its tip
- tracing face of clock and then touching it

Where?

- hand in "1" position with palm out
- shake finger from side to side
- simulating head moving from side to side looking for something

Why?

- open hand with fingertips on forehead to "Y" hand
- touch forehead and then move away from head for examination
- taking thought out and looking at it

Which?

- both hands in "10" position at chest
- hands alternate up and down
- indicating doubt (weighing options)

How?

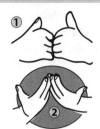

- fingers in to chest, knuckles touching
- hands flow up and out to palms facing up
- as if turning up seams to see inside edges

How much?

- both hands curved and open
- fingertips together, then apart
- showing quantity

How many?

- "S" hand with palm up
- open hand to "5" hand with palm up
- as if laying it all out to count

4 TIME, DAYS, AND TIME OF DAY

Holiday

- both hands in "5" position near armpits
- tap thumbs twice
- pulling on suspenders with nothing to do

Valentine's Day

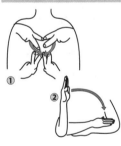

- hands in "V" position with open fingers angled down in front of chest; trace the shape of a heart with fingers
- stack right elbow on top of left hand so that arms are perpendicular; collapse right arm into left, making sign for "day"
- "V" for "valentine" + "day"

Easter

- "E" hand at shoulder
- twist hand back and forth
- "E" for Easter

Halloween

- for both hands, pointer and middle finger spread around eyes
- hands moving outward while pointer and middle finger close
- putting on a mask

Thanksgiving

- open right at hand mouth and open left hand slightly in front, palms in
- draw two arches in the air with both hands
- demonstrating gratitude or thanks

Christmas

- "C" hand in front of face
- circle hand outward so that fingers end up facing chest
- like Santa's sleigh going over the rooftops

Birthday

- open right hand on chest, palm in; left hand open, palm up, in front of chest
- right hand moves up slightly on chest, then lands in open left hand
- "happy" + "born" (**note:** may also include the sign for "day")

Time

- hand in "1" position
- tap opposite wrist
- pointing at watch

What time is it?

- hand in "1" position
- tap opposite wrist and make an inquisitive face
- common gesture for asking about the time

Watch

- right hand in "9" position resting on back of left wrist, with hand in "S" position
- —
- fingers circle face of wristwatch

Hour

- right hand in "1" position, pointer finger resting on open left hand, fingers up; both palms facing in
- make circle on palm with pointer finger
- minute hand sweeping through clock face

Minute

- starting position same as hour
- short pivot of pointer finger on palm
- minute hand moving short distance on clock face

Second

- starting position same as hour
- very short pivot of pointer finger on palm
- second hand moving very short distance on clock face

Day

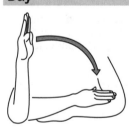

- left arm bent across body with right elbow resting in left hand; right hand flat with fingers pointing up
- right hand arcs toward left elbow
- sun moving across sky

Week

- right hand in "D" position with little finger resting on open left palm
- slide "D" hand across open palm
- moving across one week of days

Month

- hands in "1" position: left hand with pointer finger upward, palm facing right; right pointer finger touching left pointer finger toward body
- slide right finger down left finger
- one month's time

Year

- both hands in "S" position at waist, with right hand above left, palms in
- circle right hand around left, ending in starting position
- the Earth rotating around the sun

Morning

- right arm extended with palm up; left hand in crook of right arm
- right open palm moves toward face two times
- sun rising

Afternoon

- right arm, bent and extended with palm down, rests on downturned left hand
- light bounce of right arm
- sun setting

Evening

- right hand, curved with palm facing down, rests on wrist of flat left hand with palm facing down
- right wrist taps left wrist two times
- sun setting below horizon

Noon

- right arm, bent at the elbow with flat palm facing sideways, extends upward while resting on palm of left hand
- tap elbow on hand two times
- sun straight above (or hands of clock at 12:00)

Sunrise

- left arm held in front of body with palm down, right hand is in "O" position behind left arm
- right hand moves up and above left arm
- sun rising

Sunset

- left arm held in front of body with palm down, right hand is in "O" position above left arm
- right hand moves down and behind left arm
- sun setting

Now / Today

(two separate but they're the same sign)

- hands in "Y" position with palms facing in
- drop hands slightly
- —

Early

- middle finger of right hand resting on back of left hand with palm down
- tilt right hand forward
- glimpse of sun over the Earth

Late

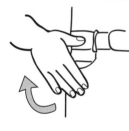

- right hand near hip with fingers down and palm back
- move hand back and forth several times
- behind

Tomorrow

- right hand in "A" position with thumb at right side of chin
- move hand up and forward
- time that is before you

Yesterday

- right hand in "Y" position with thumb at right side of chin
- move hand up and back
- time that is behind you

Forever

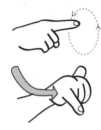

- right hand in "1" position, with pointer finger out
- make clockwise circle to audience in air and then with "Y" hand move forward in curved motion
- around the clock and into the future

Future

- open right hand with palm facing left at temple
- move hand out and up
- before you

Past

- open right hand with palm facing the body at right shoulder
- move hand back and over shoulder
- behind you

Sunday

- both hands open in front of shoulders
- each hand makes a small, repeated circular motion
- opening church doors

Monday

- "M" hand, palm out, in front of right shoulder
- circular motion with hand around vertical line
- "M" for Monday

Tuesday

- "T" hand in front of right shoulder
- circular motion with hand around vertical line
- "T" for Tuesday

Wednesday

- "W" hand with palm facing up, forearm at a 45-degree angle from upper arm
- circular motion with hand around vertical line
- "W" for Wednesday

Thursday

- "H" hand with palm facing up, forearm at a 45-degree angle from upper arm
- circular motion with hand around vertical line
- used to be signed "T" + "H"; now "H" only

Friday

- "F" hand with palm facing up, forearm at a 45-degree angle from upper arm
- circular motion with hand around vertical line
- "F" for Friday

Saturday

- "S" hand in front of right shoulder
- circular motion with hand around vertical line
- "S" for Saturday

FAMILY MEMBERS AND PEOPLE

Family

- both hands in "F" position with thumbs touching
- start with thumbs touching, then circle in outward direction until little fingers meet
- the family circle

Parents

- make "mother" shape, thumb on chin
- move hand so that thumb touches forehead, making "father" shape
- "mother" + "father"

Father

- "5" hand with thumb touching forehead
- wiggle fingers (optional)
- male signs typically made near the forehead

Mother

- "5" hand with thumb touching chin
- wiggle fingers (optional)
- female signs typically made near the chin or lower cheek

Child

- open hand, palm down
- short and repeated downward movement near waist
- patting a child on his/her head

Son

- "5" hand with thumb touching forehead
- right hand moves from male position on head to join left arm in cradle position
- rocking a male child

Daughter

- "A" hand with thumb touching chin
- right hand moves to join left arm in cradle position
- "girl" + "baby"

Baby

- arms held in cradle position
- rocking motion
- rocking an infant

Brother

- right "A" hand on right side of forehead; left hand resting at waist
- right hand joins left hand, both in "1" position
- "male" + "same"

Sister

- right "A" hand on right side of chin; left hand resting at waist
- right hand joins left hand, both in "1" position
- "female" + "same"

Uncle

- "U" hand at right side of forehead
- twist wrist back and forth a couple of times
- "U" for uncle

Aunt

- "A" hand at right side of cheek
- twist wrist back and forth a couple of times
- "A" for aunt at female region of face

Cousin

- "C" hand at forehead (male) or chin (female)
- forward twist of wrist
- "C" for cousin at male or female region of face

Husband

- right "C" hand on right side of forehead; curved left hand in front of body
- right hand joins left hand in clasp
- "man" + "marry"

Wife

- right "C" hand on right side of chin; curved left hand in front of body
- right hand joins left hand in clasp
- "woman" + "marry"

Grandfather

- right hand in "father" position; left hand open near chest
- hand makes two arcs away from body
- each arc represents one generation

Grandmother

- right hand in "mother" position
- hand makes two arcs away from body
- each arc represents one generation

Grandson

- flat "5" hand at forehead
- hand makes two arcs at forehead away from body, followed by arms in a cradle position
- "grandfather" + "baby"

Granddaughter

- thumb at chin
- flat "5" hand moves from chin away from body, pulsing twice, followed by arms in cradle position
- "grandmother" + "baby"

Boy

- flattened "C" hand on forehead
- close fingers and thumb together twice
- tipping of boy's hat (or grabbing bill on baseball cap)

Girl

- "A" hand below ear
- trace jawbone with tip of thumb, starting near ear and moving to chin
- indicating location of strings on a bonnet

Nephew

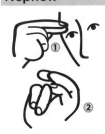

- "N" hand at right side of forehead
- forward twist of wrist
- "N" for nephew at male region of face

Niece

- "N" hand at right side of chin
- forward twist of wrist
- "N" for niece at female region of face

Man

- right hand in "boy" position with thumb touching forehead
- move hand so that thumb touches chest, palm facing down, fingers still spread
- "boy" + "fine"

Woman

- right hand in "A" position at right jaw
- thumb slides from ear to chest, fingers extending along the way
- "girl" + "fine"

Male

- thumb and fingers of right hand at forehead
- grasp imaginary cap brim
- baseball cap

Female

- right hand in "A" position at right jaw
- thumb slides from ear to chin
- traces ribbons of bonnet

5

Family Members and People

Marry

- hands clasped together in front of body, right hand on top at chest level
- —
- clasping hands in marriage

Engagement

- right hand in "E" position, palm down, touching ring finger of left hand, palm down
- —
- touching wedding ring finger

Wedding

- both hands with open palms and fingers point down at chest level
- bring right hand into left between thumb and pointer finger, left hand grasps right
- together in matrimony

Divorce

- both hands in "D" position, with palms facing inward
- quickly twist hands outward and away from each other
- "D" for divorce, indicating separation

Friend

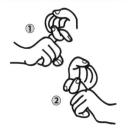

- both hands in "1" position with hooked pointer fingers linked together
- hook once, then reverse positions and hook again
- close relationship

Neighbor

- both hands in open position with right hand slightly bent
- touch palm of left hand with back of right hand, then move facing palms of both hands downward together
- "near" + "person"

Person

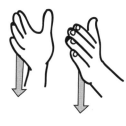

- both hands in "B" position at chest level, palms in
- move hands down along body forming body shape
- —

(**note:** this shape is often used to identify occupations)

People

- both hands in "P" position
- alternately circle them toward center
- "P" for people

5 Family Members and People

33

Sweetheart

- both hands in "A" position at chest with knuckles touching
- bend and unbend thumbs
- two people nodding to each other

I

- pointer finger of right "1" hand on chest
- —
- myself

Me

- pointer finger of right "1" hand on chest
- —
- myself

We, Us

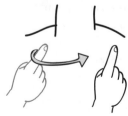

- pointer finger of right "1" hand on right shoulder
- circular motion in front to left shoulder
- pointing to self, others, and self again

You

- pointer finger of right "1" hand pointing out
- no movement for singular; move hand from left to right for plural
- natural sign

They, Them

- pointer finger of right "1" hand pointing out
- move hand toward right
- pointing to the people

She, Her

- "1" hand at chest with pointer finger pointing away from body, palm down
- jut hand forward, away from chest
- as if indicating that person

He, Him

- "1" hand at chest with pointer finger pointing away from body, palm down
- jut hand forward, away from chest
- as if indicating that person

This

- pointer finger of right "1" hand pointing down
- —
- pointing to object

That

- right hand in "Y" position resting on open left palm
- —
- —

My, Mine

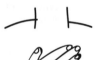

- open right palm on chest
- —
- showing possession

His, Hers

- open right hand, palm facing out
- hand pushes out
- —

Their

- open right palm faced out at chest
- move hand from left to right
- "they" + "possession"

Our

- right cupped hand facing left at right shoulder
- circular motion in front of body to left shoulder
- "we" + "possession"

Your

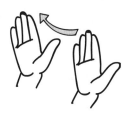

- right palm faced out
- move palm forward
- "you" + "possession"

Self/Myself

- right hand in "A" position with thumb at chest
- repeatedly strike hand on chest
- —

Ourselves

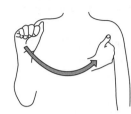

- right hand in "A" position in front of right shoulder, palm facing out
- move hand away from body in an arc while turning palm inward; hand should end up near left armpit
- —

Each, Every

- both hands in "A" position
- slide inside of right thumb over outside of left thumb one time for each, twice for every
- this handshape rubbing one's cheek indicates "every day"

Doctor

- right "D" hand with fingers resting on wrist of open left hand, palm up
- —
- "D" for doctor taking pulse

Nurse

- right "N" hand with fingers resting on wrist of open left hand, palm up
- tap right hand to wrist twice
- "N" for nurse taking pulse

Dentist

- right "D" hand with fingertips touching teeth
- tap teeth twice
- "D" for dentist working on teeth

Butcher

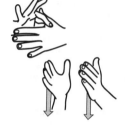

- right thumb and pointer finger pinching skin between left thumb and pointer finger; pulse twice
- —
- move hands down along body, forming body shape

Carpenter

- right hand in "S" position on top of left palm
- slide right hand forward twice, then move facing palms of both hands down together
- shaving wood

Lawyer

- right hand in "L" position on open left palm
- make small arch movement with right hand across left palm, then move facing palms of both hands downward together
- "law" + "person"

Vet

- right hand in "V" position
- fingerspelling of "V", "E", "T"
- —

Waiter

- hands at chest level, palms facing up
- right hand moves forward while left hand moves back, then move facing palms of both hands downward together
- passing dishes + "person"

Student

- right "5" hand with fingertips touching open left palm
- pull right hand upward into closed "O" shape at forward, then sign "person"
- "learn" + "person"

Teacher

- both hands in closed "O" position along sides of head
- move hands forward along head twice, then sign "person"
- "teach" + "person"

Writer

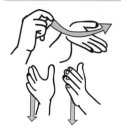

- right thumb and pointer finger pinched together while resting on open left palm, at chest level
- draw line with pinched fingers on left palm, then sign "person"
- "write" + "person"

Artist

- right "I" hand with little finger resting on open left palm at chest
- draw wavy line with lit-tle finger on left palm, then sign "person"
- "art" + "person"

Pilot

- "Y" hand at chest level
- fly "Y" away from shoulder, then sign "person"
- "fly" + "person"

Soldier

- both hands in "A" position with right above left but not touching
- tap hands twice to right side of chest, then sign "person"
- carrying a gun + "person"

Policeman

- relaxed fist with extended and curved thumb and pointer finger, both touching chest
- tap thumb and finger to chest twice
- location of badge on chest

Firefighter

- relaxed fist with extended and curved thumb and pointer finger, both touching forehead
- tap thumb and finger to forehead twice
- location of shield on helmet

King

- right hand in "K" position at left shoulder
- move hand from left shoulder to right side of waist
- forming sash

Queen

- right hand in "Q" position at left shoulder
- move hand from left shoulder to right side of waist
- forming sash

President

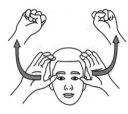

- both hands in "C" position with thumbs and pointer fingers touching temples
- move hands up and away from temples, ending in "S" position
- like hats worn by leaders in Colonial times

Priest

- right hand in relaxed "L" position at center of neck
- move hand to right side of neck
- tracing priest's collar

Nun

- both hands in "N" position on either side of head, pointer and middle fingers aligned with eyebrows
- move hands out and then down
- tracing veil

Actor

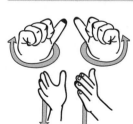

- both hands in "A" position with palms out at shoulders
- make alternate circles toward head, then sign "person"
- may be proceeded by male or female sign

Athlete

- both hands in "A" position at chest level, fingers touching
- still in "A" position, rub fingers against one another by moving wrists, then moving facing palms of both hands downward together
- —

Babysitter

- upturned right arm rests in upturned left arm
- rock arms back and forth and then change both hands to "K" position, with right resting on left
- "baby" + "keep"

Burglar

- both hands in "H" position with touching fingertips above lips
- move fingers slowly apart and then facing palms of both hands move downward together
- mustached thief + "person"

6 CLOTHING

Clothing

- both hands in "5" position touching chest below shoulders
- brush hands down across chest twice
- location of clothing

Shirt

- both hands in "F" position at chest, pinching shirt with thumbs and pointer fingers
- pinch and pull hands away twice
- indicating shirt

Sweater

- both hands in "A" position at chest level
- slide hands from chest to waist twice
- pulling on sweater

Blouse

- both hands in curved shape with thumbs touching near shoulders
- arc hands down to waist
- shape of blouse

Skirt

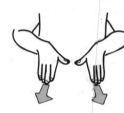

- both hands open with fingers down at hips
- move hands down two times
- location of skirt

Pants

- both hands open with fingers down below hips
- flick hands up two times
- location of pockets or pant legs

Dress

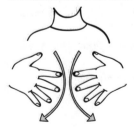

- both hands are open and resting on chest
- move both hands down simultaneously
- indicating length and shape of dress

Shoes

- both hands in "S" position with thumbs and pointer fingers touching
- tap hands together twice
- clicking heels together

Socks

- both hands in "1" position angled down in front of body
- repeatedly slide extended fingers against each other
- knitting socks

Pajamas

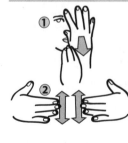

- right "5" hand in front of face
- pull right hand down over face and then rub both open hands on chest twice
- "sleep" + "clothes"

Coat

- both hands in "A" position above shoulders
- arc hands down to waist
- coat covering upper body

Hat

- **open hand** on top of head
- **pat head** twice
- **location of hat**

Gloves

- **both hands in "5" position** with palms down, right on top of left
- **slide right hand away** from fingers of left hand, then left over right
- **putting on gloves**

Umbrella

- **both hands in "S" position,** thumbs up, right above left
- **right hand moves upward** to face level
- **opening umbrella**

Button

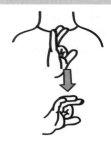

- **"F" hand** with thumb touching chest
- **touch thumb** to upper chest and then lower chest
- **thumb and forefinger** show location of buttons

Zipper

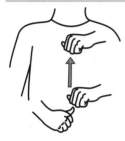

- "A" hands at the waist, right on top of left
- right hand slides up to chest
- closing a zipper

Bathrobe

- both hands in "A" position resting on chest
- rub body with closed hands and mime putting on robe
- "bath" + "robe"

7 COLORS

Color

- "5" hand at chin
- flutter fingers
- —

Red

- hand in "1" position at lips
- two downward strokes on lips, bending finger down each time
- red lips

Orange

- "C" hand in front of mouth
- squeezing motion from "C" to "S" shapes
- squeezing an orange (also sign for fruit)

Yellow

- "Y" hand in front of chest
- waving motion, bending wrist
- "Y" for yellow

Green

- "G" hand in front of chest
- waving motion, bending wrist
- "G" for green

Blue

- "B" hand in front of chest
- waving motion, bending wrist
- "B" for blue

Purple

- "P" hand in front of right shoulder
- waving motion, bending wrist
- "P" for purple

7 Colors

Black

- relaxed fist, palm down, with extended pointer finger on forehead
- pull finger from left to right across forehead
- touching (black) eyebrows

White

- "5" hand on chest
- pull hand forward while closing fingers
- touching a white shirt

Brown

- "B" hand on right cheek
- double stroke on cheek
- "B" for brown

Tan

- "T" hand on right cheek
- double stroke on cheek
- "T" for tan

Colors

7

Gray

- both hands in "5" position on chest
- move hands back and forth through open fingers
- mixing colors

Pink

- "P" hand on lips
- two downward strokes on lips with middle finger, bending finger down each time
- pink lips

8 FOOD AND MEALS

MEALS

Eat

- flattened "O" hand
- bring hand to mouth (**note:** to sign food, repeat movement)
- bringing food to mouth

Drink

- "C" hand, thumb at mouth
- tip fingers to nose
- drinking from a cup

Breakfast

- flat "O" hand at mouth
- move to extended right arm with palm up, left hand in crook of right arm; then move right open palm toward face twice
- "eat" + "morning"

Lunch

- flat "O" hand at mouth
- move to bent right arm with flat inward palm extending upward while resting on palm of left hand; bounce twice
- "eat" + "noon"

Dinner

- flat "O" hand at mouth
- move to curved right hand with palm down resting on wrist of flat left hand with palm down, making two taps of wrist of right hand on wrist of left hand
- "eat" + "night"

Restaurant

- "R" hand at mouth
- touch extended fingers first to right side and then to left side of mouth
- "R" for restaurant, at mouth

Hungry

- fingertips of "C" hand touching chest
- slide hand down chest
- digestive tract

Thirsty

- pointer finger of "1" hand on throat
- slide finger down throat
- dry throat

Menu

- extended fingers of right hand over thumb at mouth
- touch mouth twice and then move right fingertips over open left palm twice
- "eat" + "list"

Washing Dishes

- open right hand palm down on open left hand palm up
- right hand makes circular rubbing motion
- motion of washing dishes

Fork

- right hand in "W" position with left hand open, palms facing each other
- tap right hand on left palm
- tines of fork

Spoon

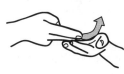

- right "H" hand, palm up, and open left hand, palm up
- small scooping motion of right hand across left palm
- spooning out of a bowl

Knife

- both hands in "1" position, palms down
- slide right extended finger across left extended finger
- sharpening knife

Plate

- both hands in "L" position, several inches apart, palms in
- —
- fingers form sides of plate

Dish

- both hands in "5" position with thumbs and middle fingers touching
- tap twice
- shape of dish

Bowl

- both hands together in cupped shape with little fingers touching
- move hands apart, ending with palms inward in "C" positions
- shape of bowl

Cup

- right "C" hand with thumb up, above extended open left hand, palm up
- move right hand toward left palm
- cup on a saucer

Glass

- right "C" hand with thumb up, resting on extended open left hand, palm up
- move right hand up off of left palm
- hand forms shape of glass

Napkin

- open right hand, palm facing in, at mouth
- wipe once on the right corner of the mouth and once on the left corner
- wiping mouth with napkin

Fruit

- "F" hand on right cheek
- double twist of fingers/wrist
- "F" for fruit

Apple

- "A" hand on right side of chin
- double twist of hand on chin
- "A" for apple; twisting stem off fruit

Orange

- "C" hand in front of mouth
- squeezing motion from "C" to "S" shapes
- squeezing an orange (**note:** also sign for color orange)

Banana

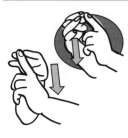

- right hand with bent fingers touching upward-extended pointer finger of left "1" hand
- move right hand down along extended finger on thumb side; repeat on opposite side
- peeling a banana

8 Food and Meals

Strawberry

- right hand fingers touching tip of left "1" hand little finger
- double twist of right hand on little finger
- picking a strawberry

Peach

- "5" hand on right cheek
- double wipe of fingers to closed "O" position across cheek
- feeling peach fuzz

Lemon

- "L" shape on chin
- double tap of thumb to chin
- "L" for lemon

Grapes

- right hand in claw shape with palm down, over left hand open with palm down
- touch right fingers to left hand while moving up arm
- bunches of grapes

Watermelon

- "W" shape at chin
- tap "W" hand twice to chin, then thump left hand with right middle finger in "8" hand shape repeatedly
- "water" + "melon"

Pear

- closed "O" of right hand around left fingers
- move right hand away from left, opening and closing fingers
- making the shape of a pear

Pineapple

- "F" shape on right cheek
- double twist of wrist
- stem of a pineapple

Coconut

- both hands in "C" position near right side of head
- shake hands twice
- shaking coconut to hear milk inside

Cherry

- right fingertips grasp pointer finger of left hand in "I" position
- twisting motion
- removing cherry from branch

Grapefruit

- both hands in "G" position
- make circular motions around each hand
- "G" for grapefruit, signed in shape of grapefruit

Berry

- fingers of right hand grasp little finger of left hand held in "1" position
- double twist of right hand
- picking a berry

Vegetable

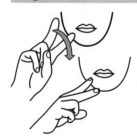

- pointer finger of "V" shape on right side of chin
- twist wrist, allowing hand to pivot on pointer finger
- "V" for vegetable

Corn

- both hands in "S" position near sides of face
- double twist of wrists together
- eating corn on the cob

Peas

- pointer finger of right "X" hand resting on pointer finger of left "1" hand with palm facing down
- move right "X" finger across left pointer finger
- touching peas in the pod

Lettuce

- curved hand along right side of forehead
- tap twice
- head of lettuce

Potato

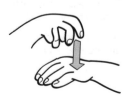

- fingers of right crooked "V" hand, palm down, above flat and extended left hand, palm down
- two taps of right hand on left hand
- testing whether a potato is done with a fork

Carrot

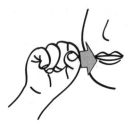

- "S" hand
- move hand slowly toward mouth, clicking teeth
- eating a carrot like a rabbit

Onion

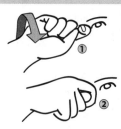

- "X" hand near right eye
- double twist of wrist
- wiping tears off eye

Celery

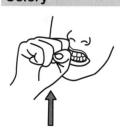

- raise hand into fist at side of mouth
- make dramatic biting motions with mouth, leaving hand where it is
- chewing on celery

Tomato

- right "1" hand near mouth with left "S" hand in front of body
- touch lips, then move right hand from mouth past left hand
- slicing a (red) tomato

Mushroom

- cupped right hand resting on left hand in "1" position with pointer finger pointed up
- —
- stem and cap of mushroom

Cabbage

- right hand bent with fingers closed, palm facing head
- gently strike head using wrist
- head of cabbage

Pickle

- middle finger of right "P" finger at right corner of mouth
- —
- "P" for pickle

Pancake

- downward open palm of right hand on upward open palm of left hand
- slap right hand on left, then flip right hand over to slap back of hand on left palm
- flipping pancakes

Bread

- slightly bent right hand above left hand extended with downward palm
- slicing motion of right hand across left hand
- slicing bread

Toast

- right "V" hand touching extended left hand with fingers up
- touch "V" to one side and then the other by rotating left hand
- holding bread with fork to toast both sides

Sandwich

- Flat left hand resting between the thumb and fingers of right hand, both hands slightly bent at knuckles
- bring hands close to mouth twice
- eating a sandwich

Cheese

- both hands open and crossed with heels of hands touching in front of body
- rub heel of right hand repeatedly across heel of left hand
- shaping cheese

Soup

- right "H" hand at mouth and open left palm facing up at chest level
- repeatedly move right hand down to left hand and up again in circular sweep
- eating soup from bowl

Pizza

- "2" hand with pointer and middle fingers extended and curved
- write "Z" in air
- "Z" for letters in pizza

Salad

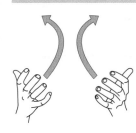

- both hands in "5" position in front of body, with fingers pointing down
- scooping motion
- tossing a salad

Beans

- fingertips of right hand are on extended pointer finger of left hand in the "1" position
- right hand fingers move up and down from knuckle to finger tip
- making the shape of a bean

Meat

- right thumb and pointer finger pinch flesh of open left hand
- shake hands together twice
- grasping meaty or fleshy part of skin

Steak

- right pointer finger and thumb on fleshy part of open left hand
- pinching motion
- fleshy part of the hand (like meat)

Hamburger

- clasped hands, right over left
- grasp left over right
- making hamburger patty

Hot Dog

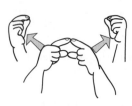

- both hands in "G" position with pointer fingers and thumbs touching in front of chest
- repeatedly pull hands apart, opening and closing pointer fingers and thumbs
- following hot dog shape

Chicken

- right "2" hand with fingers pointing down; left flat palm facing up
- right hand fingers scrape the space above left palm twice without actually touching left palm
- chicken feet

Turkey

- right hand in "G" position with thumb and pointer finger pointing down at chin
- shake right hand
- wattle of turkey

Fish

- open right hand extended forward at waist level with left fingers touching right elbow
- right hand waves side to side
- movement of fish (or fish's tail) in water

Bacon

- both hands in "H" shape touching fingertips in front of chest
- pull hands apart with slight wavy motion
- shape of bacon strips

Sausage

- hands in "C" position, pointer fingers and thumbs touching in front of chest

- repeatedly pull hands apart in front of chest, forming "S" hands during pull

- making sausage shape

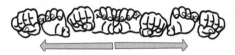

Egg

- both hands in "H" position

- bring right hand down on left hand, then move hands away from each other and down

- act of breaking egg

Spaghetti

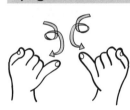

- both hands in "I" positions with little fingers touching

- move both hands apart in downward spirals

- strands of spaghetti

Noodle

- both hands in loose "I" position, pinkies touching

- make an outward arc with both hands

- —

French Fries

- "F" shape in front of chest
- shake "F" once and then again, slightly to the right
- "FF" for french fries

Rice/Grain

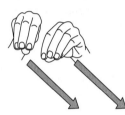

- both hands closed so that fingertips are touching thumb
- fingertips rub against one another while moving left and away from body
- planting rice/grains

Cracker

- "A" hand
- tap palm side of right hand on left elbow twice
- like cracking wheat

Dessert

- both hands with fingers touching in "D" shape in front of chest
- move hands apart two times
- "D" for dessert, coupled with sign for "more"

Sweet

- open hand on chin with palm facing in
- move hand downward over chin two times, bending fingers back toward palm each time
- as if syrup is dripping down your chin

Cake

- right hand in a claw resting on stretched left hand
- lift right hand up to chin level twice
- grabbing a piece of cake

Pie

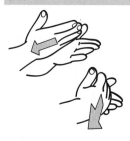

- right extended hand resting on left upward palm
- slide and twist right hand at two different angles across left palm
- simulating pie slicing

Cookie

- right hand in claw position with fingers touching left upward palm
- twist hands in opposite directions
- simulating cookie cutter

Doughnut

- both hands in "R" shape at mouth
- circle forward, bringing fingers together
- simulating shape of a doughnut

Ice Cream

- "S" hand at mouth
- repeated downward motion
- licking an ice cream cone

Chocolate

- right "C" hand, thumb resting on extended left hand with palm facing down
- circular motion of right thumb on back of left hand
- "C" for chocolate

Vanilla

- "V" hand in front of chest
- rock hand back and forth
- "V" for vanilla

8

Food and Meals

Candy

- "U" hand with pointer finger at edge of lip
- twist wrist slightly so that finger moves back and forth
- —

Chewing Gum

- right hand in "V" position with curved fingers at right cheek
- bend fingers open and closed
- chewing motion of jaw

Popcorn

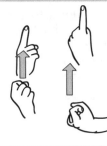

- both hands in "S" shape in front of body
- alternately flick pointer fingers while raising hands
- popcorn popping

Nuts

- "A" hand with thumb behind upper teeth
- flick thumb forward
- cracking nuts

Sugar

- tips of right pointer and middle fingers on lips
- wipe mouth with downward motion
- sweet taste on lips

Dressing/Sauce

- right hand in "A" position, thumb down
- pour sauce on food using thumb as spout
- imitates pouring action

Syrup

- right hand in "1" position with pointer finger on top lip pointing left
- wipe finger across lip from left to right twice
- wiping syrup off lip

Vinegar

- right hand in "V" position at corner of mouth
- —
- "V" for vinegar

8

Food and Meals

Ketchup

- right hand in "K" position, fingers forward
- shake up and down
- getting ketchup out of bottle

Mayonnaise

- right hand in "M" position with fingertips on open left palm
- spread "M" across palm
- "M" for mayonnaise, spreading on bread

Jelly

- right hand in "I" position with little finger on palm of left hand
- write "J"s across palm
- "J" for jelly, placed on bread

Butter

- right "U" hand on open and upward left palm
- stroke finger across palm twice
- spreading butter

Salt

- both hands in "V" position, palms down, with right "V" over left
- tap right hand on left twice
- tapping salt from salt knife

Pepper

- "9" hand with palm down
- shake twice
- using pepper shaker

Coffee

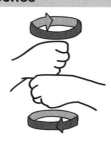

- both hands in "S" shape, with little finger of right hand touching pointer finger of left hand
- make small circles in opposite directions
- grinding coffee beans

Tea

- right hand in "F" position and left hand in "O" position, with formed "O" at top
- move fingers of right hand in and out of left hand
- dipping a tea bag

Milk

- "C" hand in front of body
- open and close to "S" shape
- milking a cow

Juice

- "J" position near mouth
- write two "J"s in the air
- "J" for juice

Soda (or Other Bubbly Drink)

- right hand in "5" position with bent middle finger in left hand in "O" position
- quickly remove middle finger, forming right hand into "5" position, then slap right hand onto left "O"
- cork popping out of a bottle

Whiskey/Liquor

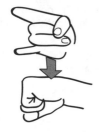

- relaxed right fist with extended pointer and little fingers above "S" left hand with palm down
- two taps of right little finger onto back of left hand
- extended right fingers show size of jigger glass

Beer

- "B" hand at right side of chin
- double stroke of hand on side of chin
- "B" for beer

Wine

- "W" hand on right cheek
- two small circles on cheek
- "W" for wine

EMOTIONS
AND
FEELINGS

Feeling

- middle finger of "5" hand on chest
- move upward on chest
- feelings come from the heart

(**note:** with the "E" handshape, this sign becomes "emotion")

Happy

- palm of open hand on chest
- move hand upward on chest twice
- feeling "up"

Sad

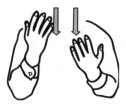

- both hands in "5" position with fingers up at sides of face
- slide hands down
- feeling "down"

Angry

- both hands in claw position with fingers toward each other at lower chest
- move hands up to shoulders
- anger "rising" in body

Tired

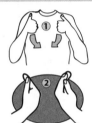

- both hands in "10" position; bent fingers on chest
- drop hands but keep little fingers on chest, thumbs resting on pointer fingers
- drop in energy

Afraid

- both hands in "5" position on chest; right hand slightly above left
- slide hands deliberately toward center of chest
- protecting body

Jealous

- "J" hand with little finger at right corner of mouth
- make small "J" shape, changing palm from outward to inward
- "J" for jealous, with a drool

Emotions and Feelings

Funny

- pointer and middle fingers of "U" hand touching nose
- slide fingers off of nose twice, bending fingers each time
- twitching nose

Embarrassed

- both hands in "5" position at sides of face
- make alternating, forward circular movements
- blush on cheeks

Frustrated

- "B" hand extended in front of mouth with angled palm facing out
- bring back of hand to mouth
- meeting obstacle

Courageous

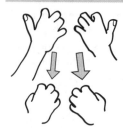

- both hands in claw position on chest
- move hands forward, changing to "S" position
- gaining strength from self

Hate/Detest

- thumbs and middle fingers of both hands are in snapping position
- flick several times
- pushing away

Like

- make "5" shape flat on chest
- draw hand away from body while closing thumb and third finger
- heart to object

Cry

- both hands in "1" position with pointer fingers at eyes
- repeatedly move fingers down cheeks
- tears on cheeks

Laugh

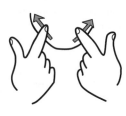

- both hands in "L" position with pointer fingers resting at corners of mouth
- repeatedly draw fingers up to cheeks
- corners of mouth turned up

9

Emotions and Feelings

Smile

- both hands in "L" position with pointer fingers resting at corners of mouth
- draw fingers up to cheeks
- smiling from ear to ear

Blush

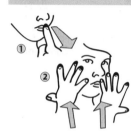

- right hand in "1" position with extended finger on lips
- brush lips and then slide both hands in "5" position up cheeks
- "red" + blushing action

Kiss

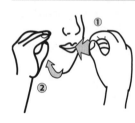

- place all fingers of right hand on lips
- move fingers from lips to cheek
- kiss on mouth and cheek

Kind/Gracious

- both hands bent with fingers closed, right over left in front of chest
- move right hand around and under left hand, then move left over and back under right
- wrapping a bandage

10 AROUND THE HOUSE

House

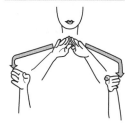

- both hands in "B" positions with fingers touching in front of forehead
- move hands apart/down at angle to shoulders, then straight down to waist
- shape of roof and walls

Home

- closed "O" at lower right cheek
- touch lower cheek, then upper cheek
- home is where you eat and sleep; house is a structure

Room

- both hands in "R" position (or "B" position) at waist level with fingers pointed out about six inches apart
- move hands from right/left position to front/back position
- four sides of room

85

Bedroom

- open right hand against right cheek
- lean head toward hand, then sign "room"
- "sleep" + "room"

Bathroom

- "T" hand in front of chest
- shake "T" back and forth
- "T" for toilet

Dining Room

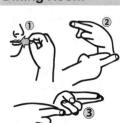

- flattened "O" hand at mouth
- touch fingers to lips, then sign "room"
- "eat" + "room"

Living Room

- right "5" hand with thumb on chest
- brush thumb upward, then sign "room"
- "fancy" + "room"

Kitchen

- right "K" hand resting on open left palm
- flip "K" on palm, then sign "room"
- "cook" + "room"

Door

- both hands in "B" shape touching in front of chest, palms out
- swing right hand back while turning left two times
- opening and closing a door

Window

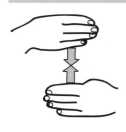

- both hands in "B" position, right above left, touching and palms in
- lift right hand twice
- opening a window

Floor

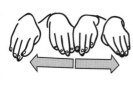

- both hands in "B" position with thumbs and pointer fingers touching, palms down, at waist level
- move hands apart on flat plane
- surface of floor

Wall

- both hands in "B" position with thumbs and pointer fingers touching, palms out, at chest level
- move hands apart along vertical plane
- surface of wall

Ceiling

- both hands in "B" position with left in front of right, palms down, above head
- bring left hand forward
- ceiling above head

Roof

- both hands in "B" positions with fingers touching in front of forehead
- move hands apart and down at angle to shoulders
- shape of roof

Stairs/Steps

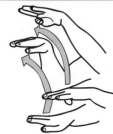

- both hands in "B" position, palms down, at waist level
- alternately move hands upward over one another
- climbing stairs

Table

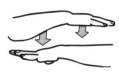

- right forearm floating above left forearm
- press right arm down to left two times
- top of table

Chair

- both hands in "U" shape, with right "U" curved over extended left "U," palms down
- tap right hand twice to left hand
- legs hanging over chair seat

Bed

- right open palm on right cheek
- lay head on palm
- head on pillow

Furniture

- right hand in "F" position in front of chest
- shake hand side to side
- "F" for furniture

Book

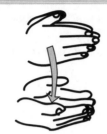

- both hands open with palms touching
- with little fingers acting as spine, open the book
- opening book

Telephone

- "Y" hand at ear
- —
- holding phone to ear

11 HEALTH AND THE BODY

Body

- both hands in open position, palms in and touching the upper chest
- touch upper chest, then lower chest
- indicating body

Head

- closed "O" position at right temple
- touch right temple, then right lower cheek
- indicating head

Nose

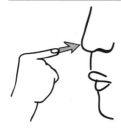

- "1" hand at nose
- touch pointer finger to nose
- indicating nose

Ear

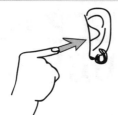

- "1" hand at ear
- touch pointer finger to ear
- indicating ear

Mouth

- "1" hand at mouth
- circle mouth with pointer finger
- location and shape of mouth

Lips

- "1" hand at lips
- touch pointer finger to lips
- indicating lips

Tongue

- "1" hand at tongue
- touch pointer finger to tongue
- indicating tongue

Teeth

- "1" hand at teeth
- touch pointer finger to teeth
- indicating teeth

Face

- "1" hand at right cheek
- make circle around face with pointer finger
- shape of face

Hair

- "F" hand holding a few strands of hair with thumb and pointer finger
- —
- indicating hair

Beard

- open fingers and thumb of right hand on chin
- draw hand down while closing fingers
- indicating location of beard

Arm

- curve "5" hand on opposite upper arm
- move hand repeatedly over upper arm
- indicating arm

Hands

- open hands with palms in at chest level
- wipe right hand on back of left hand, then reverse
- indicating hands

Feet

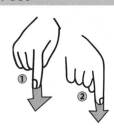

- hand in "1" position with pointer finger down
- point to one foot, then the other
- indicating feet

Bones

- both hands in curved "V" position, curved at wrists, facing signor
- —
- skeleton's crossed bones

Cold

- modified "9" hand with pinched pointer finger and thumb on nose
- double downward movement pinching pointer finger and thumb together each time
- wiping nose

Sick

- both hands in "5" position; right middle finger bent, touching forehead; left middle finger bent, touching lower chest
- —
- sick in head and stomach

Headache

- both hands in "1" position at forehead with palms down
- short movements of pointer fingers toward each other twice
- hurt near head

Temperature/Fever

- both hands in "1" position with left pointer finger touching behind right pointer finger in upright position
- slide left pointer finger up and down on right pointer finger
- mercury in thermometer

Injection

- pointer finger of right "L" hand near upper left bent arm
- touch pointer finger to arm while lowering right thumb
- giving an injection

Pill

- "8" shape in front of mouth
- flick middle finger against thumb
- putting pill in mouth

Operation

- right hand in "A" position with extended thumb on the fingertips of extended left hand, palm up
- slide thumb up palm (**note:** same motion can be done on operated part of body)
- making an incision

Blind

- bent "V" hand at eyes
- move fingers toward eyes
- shutting out the eyes

Deaf

- right pointer finger below ear
- move finger in a straight line to edge of lip
- indicating hearing and speech

Hard of Hearing

- right hand in "H" position with fingers pointing forward
- fingerspell a lowercase "h"
- an "H" and an "h" for hard of hearing

Hearing Aid

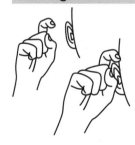

- make "X" shape near ear
- twist hand twice in backward direction
- putting hearing aid mold in ear

Hearing

- right hand in "1" position with pointer finger pointing left at mouth
- roll finger forward in circular motion
- hearing words tumbling from mouth

Glasses

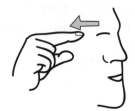

- right hand in closed "L" position at temple with fingers pointing forward
- move hand from temple to ear
- outlining frame of glasses

Pregnant

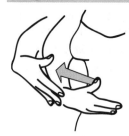

- curved "5" hand held near stomach area
- move hand away from body
- indicating size and shape of pregnant belly

Born/Birth

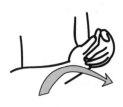

- upturned right hand on stomach and upturned left hand in front of stomach
- bring right hand forward to left hand
- from the womb

Die/Death

- both hands are open with fingers pointing forward with right hand palm down and left hand palm up
- flip hands
- turning over

Sleep

- right hand in "5" position with palm toward face
- draw hand down toward chin while closing fingers
- eyes closing

Awaken

- both hands in closed "L" position at sides of eyes
- open and close pointer fingers and thumbs
- eyes opening

Heart

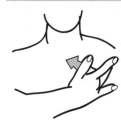

- middle finger of right hand touches heart area of chest
- —
- location of heart

Healthy

- both hands in "5" position on chest near shoulders
- move hands away from chest while closing into "S" position
- strong body

12 MONEY

Money

- right hand in flattened "O" position with palm floating up above open left hand, palm up
- tap right hand to left palm twice
- laying money on hand

Buy

- back of right hand in flattened "O" position, resting on open left palm
- move right hand forward in arc
- giving money to another

Pay

- pointer finger of right hand in "1" position, touching open left palm
- sweep right hand across left palm to beyond fingertips
- paying off what is owed

Sell

- flattened "O" hands in downward position at chest
- move fingertips back and forth from wrists
- holding item for sale

Price

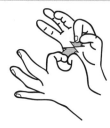

- both hands in "9" position with thumbs and pointer fingers touching
- tap fingers twice
- —

Coin

- right hand in "F" shape above open left palm
- make three chops with right hand against left palm
- shape of coin held in hand

Penny

- "1" position at right forehead
- two short movements forward
- —

Nickel

- pointer finger touching forehead
- draw hand away from forehead while opening hand up to a "5" shape
- "5" as in five cents

Dime

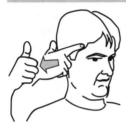

- "1" position at right forehead
- two short movements forward, changing the "1" into a "10" with a wiggle
- —

Quarter

- "1" position at right forehead
- two short movements forward, changing "1" into "5"; pointer and middle fingers bent and wiggling
- —

Dollar Bill

- right hand grasping pointer finger side of open left hand, palm in
- slide right hand along left, ending in a "10" position
- —

Dollar (amount)

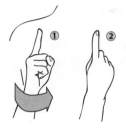

- "1" position, palm out
- twist wrist, ending with palm in
- "1" + dollar twist (**note:** can sign number + twist for amounts up to $10)

Credit Card

- right hand in "S" position; extended little finger resting on open left palm
- slide right little finger back/forth across palm
- simulating sliding action of machine reading a credit card

Check

- place fingertips of right "C" hand on open left palm
- move right hand across palm toward left fingertips
- "C" for check, signed in the size of a check

Rich

- right hand in flattened "O" position with palm up above left hand, palm up
- lift right hand up while opening it, ending with palm facing down
- pile of money

Poor

- place fingers of open right hand on left elbow
- pull down repeatedly
- worn materials at elbows

Expensive

- right hand in flattened "O" position with palm up above left hand, palm up
- lift right hand up while opening it and throwing imaginary contents to right
- —

Cheap

- place pointer finger of right open hand on pointer finger of left open hand, palm up
- slide right pointer finger across left fingers
- —

NATURE
AND THE
WEATHER

Winter

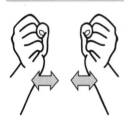

- both hands in "S" position with palms facing each other at sides of chest
- shake repeatedly
- shivering (same as cold)

Spring

- left hand grasping closed "O" right hand with extended fingers pointing up
- slide right hand upward to form "5" hand, palm in
- plant sprouting

Summer

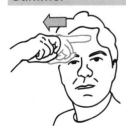

- pointer finger of "1" hand on forehead with palm down
- slide finger across forehead, changing to an "X" hand
- wiping sweat off brow

Autumn

- right "B" hand with palm down at elbow of bent left arm
- double downward movement of right hand
- falling leaves

Weather

- both hands in "W" position with extended fingers touching in front of chest
- twist wrists twice
- "W" for "changing" weather

Rain

- hands in claw position with palms down in front of shoulders
- double downward movement of hands
- falling raindrops

Snow

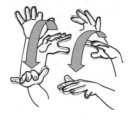

- both hands in "5" position with palms down in front of shoulders
- fluttering of fingers as hands lower to chest level
- falling snowflakes

Wind

- both hands in "5" position with palms in and fingers up in front of chest
- simultaneous arcs two times
- moving air

Storm

- both hands in "5" position with one palm in, one palm out, with fingers pointing in same direction
- wave hands simultaneously from side to side
- quickly moving air

Cloud

- make "C" shape with both hands
- twist hands away from one another while moving arms to the left
- shape of clouds

Sun

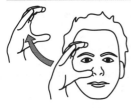

- make "C" shape around eye
- move hand away from forehead in swooping motion
- —

Moon

- curved fingers of "L" hand at eye
- —
- crescent shape of the moon

Tornado

- both hands in "1" position, with left pointer finger pointed up at chest level and right finger pointing down at shoulder level
- spiral right hand up
- shape of tornado

Hurricane

- both hands in open claw position, with left fingers pointed up at chest level and right fingers pointing down at shoulder level
- spiral left hand up
- whipping hurricane winds

Flood

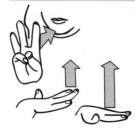

- pointer finger of "W" hand touching chin
- tap chin twice; then both hands in "5" position, with palms down at chest level, raise up twice
- "water" + "rising"

Rainbow

- right "4" hand with palm facing in and fingers pointing to left
- arc hand to upright position
- colors and shape of rainbow

Stars

- both hands in "1" position with pointer fingers touching, palms facing out
- alternately slide sides of fingers together while moving hands upward
- twinkling stars

Freeze/Frozen

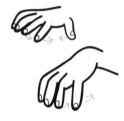

- both hands in claw position with palms facing down
- short, repeated, stiff motion of fingers
- frozen in position

Water

- right hand in "W" position with pointer finger at right corner of mouth
- strike repeatedly
- "W" for water, drinking near mouth

Lightning

- right hand in "1" position with pointer finger upward
- make zigzag motion
- flash of lightning

Thunder

- right hand in "1" position
- point to right ear and then alternately move both hands in "S" position at chest level
- vibrations of thunder

Earthquake

- rest thumb and pointer fingers of right hand in "F" position on back of left hand
- rock right hand back and forth and then alternately move both hands in "S" position at chest level
- "earth" + "thunder"

River

- right hand in "W" position with pointer finger at right corner of mouth
- with palms down, move open left hand behind right hand toward right with fingers wiggling
- "water" + "movement"

Ocean

- right hand in "W" position with pointer finger at right corner of mouth
- with palms down, move curved left hand behind right hand toward right while making waving motion
- "water" + "waves"

Tree/Forest

- place elbow of right arm in left hand while extending right hand upward in "5" position
- shake right hand rapidly
- leaves in trees

Flower

- place fingertips of right hand at right nostril
- move to left nostril
- smelling a flower

14 OPPOSITES

Good

- hand open, palm in, at mouth
- move hand away from mouth
- offering something that tastes good

Bad

- hand open, palm in at mouth
- twist hand while moving it away from mouth, ending with palm down
- discarding something that tastes bad

Fast

① ②

- both hands in "1" position with pointer fingers extended forward
- pull hands to chest quickly, forming "S" hands
- show fast-moving action

Slow

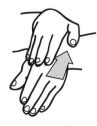

- both hands in "B" position with palms down, right on top of left
- slowly pull fingers of right hand back over fingers of left hand
- show slow-moving action

Large

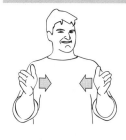

- both hands in "L" position with palms facing one another at chest level
- move hands apart as though stretching a rubber band
- "L" for large; showing large size

Small

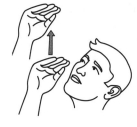

- both hands in open position at chest, palms facing in with fingers out, at shoulder width
- move hands toward each other twice
- showing small size

Tall

- fingers bent, pointing toward cheek
- raise hand above head, fingers still in bent position
- showing height

Short

- bent "B" hand with palm down at chest height
- single short downward movement
- indicates short height

Right

- both hands in "1" position with fingers extended forward and angled inward, right finger above left finger
- tap twice
- —

Wrong

- "Y" hand at chin, palm in
- tap twice
- —

New

- both hands open with palms up at waist level, right above left, with right off-center
- sweep right hand in arc across left hand
- scooping up something new

Old

- "C" hand palm down at chin
- bring hand down to waist, changing to "S" position
- stroking a beard

Hot

- curved "5" hand with palm toward mouth
- twist hand while moving it away from mouth, ending with palm down
- throwing hot item from mouth

Cold

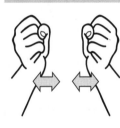

- both hands in "S" position with palms facing each other at chest level
- shake hands back and forth
- shivering motion

Same

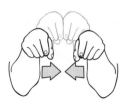

- both hands in "1" position, pointer fingers extended out at chest level
- move hands together until pointer fingers touch
- bringing like items together

14

Opposites

Different

- both hands in "1" position; pointer fingers extended out at angle and crossed at chest level
- swing hands apart
- separating unlike items

Easy

- both hands in bent "B" shape, palms up, with left fingertips atop right fingertips
- right fingertips brush up twice against left fingertips; left hand is stationary
- showing ease

Difficult

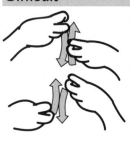

- both hands in bent "V" position, palms in, at chest level
- strike knuckles against each other twice in alternate directions
- two hard objects hitting each other

Quiet

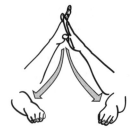

- both hands in "B" position, palms facing in and crossed in front of mouth
- move hands down and apart, still in "B" position
- —

Loud

- both hands in "5" position with pointer fingers near ears
- move away and down from ears with fluttering motion
- —

With

- both hands in "A" position with palms touching
- —
- indicating connection

Without

- both hands in "A" position with palms touching
- open and separate hands
- —

Start

- right hand in "1" position with pointer finger on open left palm between pointer and middle fingers
- make half a small circle at pointer and middle fingers
- turning a key

Stop

- both hands in open position with right palm facing left and left palm facing up
- strike left palm sharply with right little finger
- creating barrier

Right (direction)

- right hand in "R" position
- move to the right
- directional

Left (direction)

- right hand in "L" position
- move to left
- directional

Before

- both hands in open position with palms toward body, thumbs up, and left palm resting on back of right hand
- draw right hand away from left and toward body
- indicating the past

After

- both hands in open position with palms toward body, thumbs up, and right palm resting on back of left hand
- move right hand away from left hand and body
- forward movement

Ahead

- both hands in "A" position facing each other
- move right "A" in front of left "A"
- —

Behind

- both hands in "A" position facing each other
- move right "A" behind left "A"
- —

Light

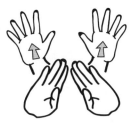

- both hands in open position with palms facing out and pointer fingers touching
- move hands up and to the side, ending in "5" position
- rays of light

Dark

- both hands in open position with palms facing face
- cross hands in front of face
- showing darkness

Together

- both hands in "A" position with knuckles touching
- move hands together to the right, forward, and left "A" in semicircle
- indicating in tandem

Apart

- both hands are curved with palms down and finger backs touching
- pull hands apart
- separation

15 ANIMALS

Animal

- open bent hands on either side chest
- slide hands in while keeping fingers in the same place (twice)
- —

Dog

- hand in "B" position with fingers down along thigh
- tap thigh twice
- calling a dog (**note:** can also snap fingers after tapping thigh)

Cat

- "F" hands on cheeks with palms facing each other
- move hands to side away from mouth
- whiskers

Horse

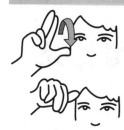

- right hand in "3" position with extended thumb touching side of head
- move fingers up and down twice
- horse ears

Bird

- right hand is in closed "L" position with touching thumb and pointer finger in front of mouth
- open and close thumb and pointer finger
- bird's beak

Snake

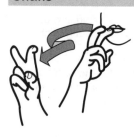

- "V" position with pointer finger near mouth
- move hand away from mouth in wavy motion
- fangs of snake

Bear

- both hands in "5" position with palms down near opposite shoulders
- scratch fingers on chest
- bear hug

15

122

Monkey

- both hands in "5" position near the armpits with palms up
- scratch in upward direction twice
- scratching movement of monkey

Deer

- both hands in "5" position above temples
- —
- antlers of a buck

Mouse

- "1" position with pointer finger on right side of nose
- flick finger across nose twice
- twitching of mouse's nose

Turtle

- left hand with palm down covering right in "A" position
- wiggle thumb
- turtle's head

Frog

- "S" hand below chin with fingers on left
- flick pointer and middle fingers to a "U" position
- movement of croaking frog's throat

Duck

- touched fingers of "3" hand with back of hand touching mouth
- open and close fingers twice
- movement of duck's bill

Bee

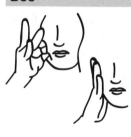

- "8" hand to right cheek
- open hand to flat palm and gently pat cheek
- a sting and a slap

Elephant

- back of open hand touching nose
- move hand away from nose in wavy motion
- trunk of elephant

Giraffe

- both hands in "C" position, palms toward body, with right on top of left in front of neck
- move right hand upward and above head
- neck of giraffe

Butterfly

- both hands open with palms up, wrists crossed, thumbs linked
- flutter fingers repeatedly
- butterfly wings

Spider

- both hands in claw position with palms down and wrists crossed
- wiggle fingers repeatedly
- spider's legs

Mule/Donkey

- one or both open hands with palms forward at side(s) of head
- open and close hands
- ears of donkey

Cow

- one or both "Y" hands with thumb(s) at side(s) of head
- keeping thumb(s) on head, twist little finger(s) upward
- horns of cow

Pig

- place back of open right hand under chin
- repeatedly bend hand
- full like a pig

Sheep

- place right hand in "2" position with palm up on extended left arm with closed hand palm down
- make shearing motion with right hand moving from wrist to elbow
- shearing a sheep

Rabbit

- both hands in "H" position, with wrists crossed
- repeatedly bend fingers
- rabbit ears

Squirrel

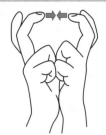

- both hands in bent "V" positions, palms toward each other
- touch knuckles together repeatedly
- front paws of squirrel

Skunk

- right hand in "K" position, with extended fingers pointing downward and thumb on forehead
- move hand from forehead to back of head
- stripe of skunk

Alligator

- both hands in "5" position with palms together, fingers forward, and one hand on top of the other
- open and close hands
- jaws of alligator

Beaver

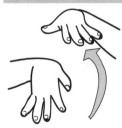

- both hands in open position with palms down, left over right
- repeatedly strike back of right hand against left palm
- tail of beaver

15 Animals

Porcupine

- both hands in "S" position with right hand resting on back of left

- move right hand down fingers of left while extending right hand to "5" position

- quills of porcupine

Pet

- both hands in open position with palm of right hand resting on back of left hand

- stroke back of left hand with right hand

- stroking pet

16 SPORTS

Football

- both hands in "5" position with palms facing each other
- repeatedly interlock fingers
- clashing

Volleyball

- both hands in open position with palms away from body
- hit imaginary volleyball
- volleying a ball

Baseball

- both hands in "S" position with right atop left
- move arms back into an imaginary bat swinging position
- swinging bat

Basketball

- both hands at bent "5" position, right palm facing forward, left palm facing up
- shoot an imaginary basketball
- shape of basketball

Soccer

- both hands in "B" position with right hand above left hand
- strike right little finger down on left pointer finger
- kicking motion

Boxing

- both hands in "S" position
- make boxing motions
- —

Hockey

- right hand in "X" position with back of crooked pointer finger resting on open left palm
- repeatedly scrape pointer finger across palm
- hockey stick scraping over ice

Golf

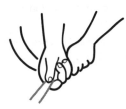

- both hands in "S" position with thumbs away from body and with right in front of left
- hold an imaginary golf club
- —

Tennis

- right hand in "S" position
- hold imaginary tennis racket and serve
- tennis swing

Skiing

- both hands in "X" position in front of right shoulder
- move hands downward and then up and to the right, creating a hook shape in the air
- going down a steep slope

Bowling

- right hand in curved "5" position
- hold imaginary bowling ball and roll it forward
- bowling ball

16

Sports

Bicycle

- both hands in "S" position with palms down
- alternately circle hands forward
- pedaling motion

Horseback Riding

- sign for "horse," then straddle pointer and middle fingers of right "V" hand over pointer finger side of left open palm
- move both hands up, down, and forward
- riding a horse

Swimming

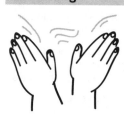

- both hands in open position in front of body
- move hands in a natural swimming motion
- —

Fishing

- both hands in relaxed "A" positions
- make quick upward motions with wrists
- pulling up a line

Jogging

- both hands in relaxed "A" positions
- make jogging action with bent elbows
- natural motion

Exercise

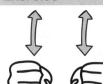

- both hands in "S" position above shoulders
- move hands up and down
- lifting weights

Gym

- both hands in "S" position with palms down in front of body
- move hands back and forth and then up and down
- calisthenic exercises

17 TRANSPORTATION AND PLACES

Boat

- both hands are cupped and together with palms up
- move hands forward in bobbing motion
- hull of boat in water

Train

- both hands in "U" position with palms down and right atop left
- move right "U" back and forth over left "U"
- train tracks

Plane

- right hand in "I love you" position
- move hand up and away from body
- wings of airplane

Car

- both hands in "A" position grasping imaginary steering wheel
- make driving motions with hands
- steering a car (**note:** also sign for "to drive")

Tent

- pointer fingers and little fingers touching; other fingers curled inward with thumbs touching third and fourth finger
- hands pull away from each other and then down once they've reached shoulder width
- shape of tent

Community

- both hands in "B" position with fingertips touching and arms forming triangular shape
- repeatedly separate and rejoin fingertips while moving arms slightly to left and to right
- many rooftops

School

- both hands in open position, with left palm up and right palm down
- repeatedly clap hands together
- teaching; getting attention

College

- both hands in open position, with left palm up and right palm down
- right hand swings up in an arc over left
- higher schooling

Library

- right hand in "L" position with palm up
- make small circular motion
- "L" for library

Church

- right hand in "C" position resting on back of left hand in "S" position
- lift right hand and place on back of left
- "C" for church on firm foundation

City

- both hands in "B" position with fingertips touching and arms forming triangle shape
- repeatedly separate and rejoin fingertips while moving arms slightly to left and to right
- many rooftops

Farm

- "5" hand with thumb underneath left side of chin
- trace thumb along chin so that hand ends up on right side of face
- like a farmer's beard

Country

- fingers of right hand rest on left elbow
- right hand makes continuous circles on elbow
- rough elbows for roughing it in country

Hospital

- right hand in "H" position on upper left arm
- trace cross with fingers
- red cross on sleeve

Museum

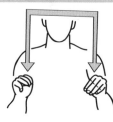

- both hands in "M" position at eye level
- move hands to trace roof and walls
- "M" for museum, indicating building

Post Office

- right hand in "P" position
- followed by right hand in "O" position
- fingerspelling "PO"

Road

- both hands in "B" position with palms facing each other
- move hands together in winding motion away from body
- winding road

Neighborhood

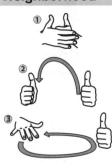

- right palm flat against left thumbs-up hand; right hand pulls away in an upward arc, ending in a thumbs-up position parallel to left hand
- right flat palm traces a circle going away from body; left hand doesn't move
- indicating an enclosed area

17

18 COMMON AND USEFUL WORDS

Awake

- extended pointer fingers and thumbs of both hands on closed eyelids
- slowly separate fingers while opening eyes
- "opening eyes"

Perfect

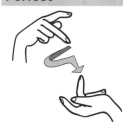

- both hands in "P" position with right above left
- circle right hand above left, ending with middle fingers touching
- "P" for perfect

Famous

- both hands in "1" position with pointer fingers on each side of mouth, palms in
- move hands outward in two arcs
- forming a (famous person) moustache

Common

- hand in "Y" position with palm down at chest level
- make repeated small circles
- —

Favorite

- "5" hand with bent middle finger on chin
- tap twice to chin
- —

Careful

- both hands in "V" position with right above left, palms facing each other at chest
- tap right hand to left twice
- combination of "watch" + "warn"

Interesting

- both hands in "5" position with bent middle fingers touching chest, right hand above left
- pull hands away from chest, pinching middle fingers to thumbs
- —

Fancy

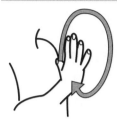

- "5" hand with thumb against chest
- slide thumb up on chest and away from body with thumb touching chest twice
- —

Polite

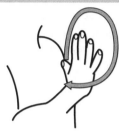

- "5" hand with thumb against chest
- slide thumb up on chest and away from body, creating a large circle with thumb touching chest twice
- smaller version of "fancy"

Secret

- "A" hand with thumb in front of chin
- tap thumb twice to chin
- lips are sealed

Important

- both hands in "F" position, palms up, little fingers almost touching
- make vertical circle, ending with thumbs and pointer fingers touching
- —

Know

- right fingertips on forehead
- pat fingertips
- information in brain

To Not Know

- right fingertips on forehead
- pat fingertips and then turn right hand away from head
- "know" + "not"

Remember

- both hands in "A" position with right thumb on forehead and left hand in front of chest
- bring right thumb down to meet left thumb
- memory continues

Forget

- right open hand on forehead with fingers pointing left
- slide hand across forehead ending in an "A" position
- erased from mind

Memorize

- pointer finger of right "1" hand on forehead
- draw hand away from forehead into "S" position
- grasping a thought

Hug

- cross arms across chest
- —
- natural hug

To Dress

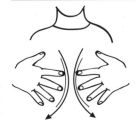

- both hands in "5" position on chest
- repeatedly move hands down over clothing
- —

Draw

- right hand in "I" position with little finger resting on open left vertical palm
- trace line on palm
- pencil drawing on paper

Cook

- both hands in open position with right palm resting in upturned left palm
- flip right hand from palm down to palm up
- flipping a pancake

Write

- right hand grasps imaginary pencil while resting on open left vertical palm
- write across palm
- pencil writing on paper

Read

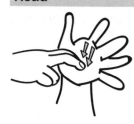

- place extended fingers of right "V" hand on palm of open left "5" hand
- move right fingers across palm
- scanning the page

See

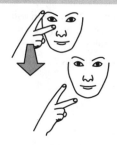

- place extended fingers of right "V" hand next to eyes
- move hand away from face
- eyes seeing

Dance

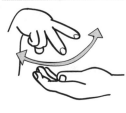

- right hand in downturned "V" position with extended fingers floating above upturned left palm
- swing "V" fingers back and forth
- legs dancing

Climb

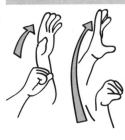

- both hands in front of chest with palms out
- hands simulate hand-over-hand climbing motion
- climbing ladder

Walk

- both hands in open position with palms down
- alternately move hands forward and backward
- movement of feet

Travel

- right hand bent in "V" shape
- right hand moves up and to the left in a big arch
- going from one place to another

Fly

- right hand in "Y" position
- move hand up and away from body
- wings of airplane

Break

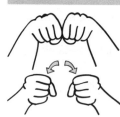

- both hands side by side in "S" position with touching thumbs and pointer fingers
- move hands apart while breaking imaginary object in two
- breaking object

Listen

- Right hand in "C" position around ear
- —
- ears hearing

Bring

- both hands in open position with palms up at chest
- move hands together from left to right
- carrying an object

Hit

- right hand in "A" position (fist) and left hand open with palm to right
- strike right hand into left
- natural sign

Say

- pointer finger of right "1" hand pointing left at mouth
- pointer finger moves outward, away from chin
- words from mouth

Sign

- hands in "D" positions with pointer fingers pointing toward chest
- hands make circular pedaling motion in front of chest
- same as "sign language"

Teach

- fingertips of both hands at temples
- move fingertips forward and backwards twice quickly
- from the mind

Grow

- right hand at waist level with palm down
- lift hand up to shoulder
- getting taller

Stand

- right hand in downturned "V" position with extended fingers resting on upturned left palm
- —
- two legs standing

Fall

- right hand in downturned "V" position with extended fingers resting on upturned left palm
- flip right hand over to back of right hand resting on left palm
- act of falling

Lie (down)

- right hand in "V" position with palm up resting on upturned left palm
- —
- lying down

Get Up

- right hand in "V" position with palm toward body with open left hand extended palm up
- swing right hand over to rest pointer and middle fingers on left palm
- onto one's feet

Jump

- right hand in downturned "V" position with extended fingers resting on upturned left palm
- raise hand quickly and repeatedly
- legs jumping

Sit

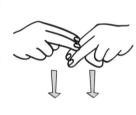

- both hands in "H" position with pointer and middle fingers of right hand draped over pointer and middle fingers of left hand
- repeatedly move hands downward slightly
- legs over chair

Run

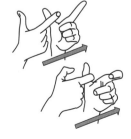

- both hands in "L" position, right pointer finger touching left thumb
- both hands move upwards and to the right as pointer fingers flex twice
- —

Drive

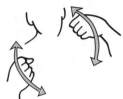

- both hands in "A" position grasping imaginary steering wheel

- make driving motions with hands

- steering a car (**note:** also sign for "car")

Make

- both hands in "S" position with right hand atop left

- strike hands together while twisting them in opposite directions

- making something with hands

Common and Useful Words

18

INDEX

Index

154